Writing for Audiobooks: Audio-First for Flow & Impact

Author Advice from Radio Writing

JULES HORNE

Interested in publishing an audiobook? This primer on radio writing techniques will transform your writing and editing for the voice-first market.

For more on voice-first writing, visit
www.method-writing.com

Copyright © 2020 by Jules Horne. All rights reserved.

Texthouse, The Corn Exchange, Woodmarket, Kelso, TD5 7AT
www.texthouse.co.uk

Writing for Audiobooks: Audio-First for Flow & Impact / Jules Horne. — 1st ed.

Cover design: Victor Marcos
www.99designs.com/profiles/victormarcos/services

ISBN
978-1-9164960-1-9 (paperback)
978-1-9164960-0-2 (ebook)

Contents

Introduction	ix
So, Who's This Book For?	x
How to Use This Book	xii
A Bit About Me	xiii

CHAPTER 1 — 1

What's Different About Audio?	3
New to Audio? Five Key Concepts	3
Firstly: eyes versus ears	
Two: listening is linear	
Three: visuals and layout	
Four: writing flow and structure	
Finally, the power of performance	
Frequently Asked Questions	4
Is audio-first writing complicated?	
Can I leave it up to my narrator?	
Do I need this? I'm a literary writer	
What's new? I'm a natural born storyteller	
Is audio-first useful for fiction?	
Is this useful for non-fiction?	
What do you suggest for writers in a hurry?	
Will this help with narrating my own book?	
Audio-First Writers	6
Early Storytelling	7
Modern Storytellers	8
Performing artists	
Broadcast journalists	

    Scriptwriters for radio, stage or screen
    Preachers, orators, politicians
Audiobook Research   9

CHAPTER 2   11

Audio and Listening   13
The Audio Medium   13
    Technology
    How to ensure audio quality?
    Platform
    What does Whispersync mean for writers?
Listeners   17
    Human variation

CHAPTER 3   19

Visual Book Elements   21
Large Graphics   21
Statistics and Graphs   22
Numbers   23
Structural Elements   24
    Titles and section headers
    Bullet points & lists
Typography   25
Quote marks and dialogue   25
Web Elements   26

CHAPTER 4   27

Writing for Flow   29
What is Flow?   30
    Writing Techniques
Getting Attention - Openings   31
    Introductory words
    Attunement
    Attunement in fiction
    Three key elements
    Opening edits

    Opening words - non-fiction
Sustaining Attention - Middles   40
    Spans
    Flow and the Zeigarnik Effect
    Forward flagging
    Backward flagging
    Repetition and touches
Foregrounding   46
    Pattern and disruption
    Intensity and power words
    Nouns
    Verbs
Signposts and Order of Information   51
    Sentence length
    "Which", brackets, dashes
    Tenses
Endings   55
    Landing
    Summary words

CHAPTER 5   59

Writing for Audience Impact   61
Narrative Viewpoint   62
    Direct address "you"
    Contractions
    Register

CHAPTER 6   67

Into the Studio   69
Test Your Script   69
Working with a Narrator   70
Finding a Narrator   71
Preparation to Help Your Narrator   72
    Layout
    Pronunciation
    Emphases

Narrating Your Own Book	74
Editing for Your Own Narration	76
Work on paper	
Tricky expressions	
Resonant sounds	
Speaking - Voice Energy, Projection, Speed, Accents	78
Voice energy and projection	
Speed perception	
Accents	
Recording Tips	80
Clean capture	
Your recording space	
About echo	
Acoustic treatment	
Microphone placement	
And Finally	85
What's Next?	86
Get Your Free Ebook	87
About Jules Horne	88
Other Books by Jules Horne	89

Introduction

Audiobooks are enjoying an exciting boom, and it's set to continue and grow.

More and more people are listening to audiobooks in preference to reading. Major publishers are reporting 20-30% increases in audiobook sales. And some are commissioning straight-to-audio fiction.

So if you're a writer, this is a big deal. The book market is shifting towards audio, and you need to be part of it.

However, not every book is great for audio. Not every writer knows about audio writing techniques. Those that do will find their books make an easy transition. The writing will be more fun for narrators to read, and clearer and more compelling for listeners to hear.

Writing for the ear calls for specific skills. Skills that are well known in the worlds of radio, performance, and spoken word. But far less familiar in the world of traditional books.

Since audiobooks are on the rise, it makes sense for writers to learn those skills, and soon.

I'm particularly excited because I'm a fiction writer with a professional background in radio. I've written for stage, and performed spoken word in English and Scots. The rhythms and music of spoken word are in my writing DNA anyway.

And suddenly, the extra techniques I've learned from radio and stage writing have turned out to be very useful indeed.

They're easy to learn, and they'll transform your impact as an audiobook author.

You may even decide to join the many authors now writing with audio-first in mind.

This is a handbook for anyone interested in audio writing – writing for the ear, writing for performance.

If you're traditionally published, you'll learn audio writing strategies and be well prepared for this growing and lucrative market.

If you're an indie author, you'll learn how to prepare your books for audio recording and what to consider when working with a narrator or narrating your own book.

I'll be covering, among other things:

- How do you write for the audio platform?
- What's different about writing for the ear, rather than the eye?
- How do you deal with visual elements such as URLs, images, graphs, tables, headers?
- Can audio-first writing improve your book for listeners?

The answer is "yes". Of course!

The written and spoken word are very different media, as you'll discover. And audio is tremendous fun!

So, Who's This Book For?

Anyone who wants to up their writing game, and polish their books for better audio impact.

Fiction authors – both traditionally published and indie – who are interested in this booming market for storytellers.

INTRODUCTION

Non-fiction authors wondering how to adapt their books for audio.

Teachers of professional writing who want an overview of audio-specific writing skills.

Early adopters excited by audiobooks. Hopefully, that's you!

But first, a story.

I was a young, newly published fiction writer. I'd even won a prize and was feeling pretty pleased with myself. And I'd just written my first playscript, and was in my first rehearsal, waiting for my beautiful words to be beautifully read by actors.

So I was shocked by what happened next.

The actors – very experienced and one even rather famous – were running out of breath. My lines were too long. Full of qualifying clauses. Piled-on adjectives. Some bits weren't even quite logical.

Now, I'd worked very hard on that script. It was well written, and well edited. But as a script for performance, it didn't work.

Wow - did I sharpen up after that! Every word had to be weighed and counted.

An audiobook is a script. Your narrator makes it a performance. And that alone calls for different writing skills.

So, some of what follows comes from the world of performance. Some of it comes from my BBC training in radio news. Some of it comes from teaching many aspiring and inspiring writers as a tutor for the Open University.

Most of the techniques are straightforward, and you can put them into practice right away. I've gathered some of the main ones in a download on my website – see the link at the end of this book.

Others go deeper into what's different about ears, linear thinking and audio flow – including hooks and arcs that keep things moving forward.

Rest assured: you don't need to change your writing voice – simply get some extra editing and structuring skills to help listeners who'll hear your story only once. Skills that are great, as it happens, for your editing in general.

Audio offers an amazing sense of connection. The intimacy of voices in your ear, the music, rhythm and humanity of different and distinctive ways of telling stories.

You may find that the spoken word is more natural for you, and your writing can flourish in audio form.

If you already write spoken word, performance poetry, dialect or scripts, maybe audiobooks are your natural home!

Audio is different.

Publishers, readers and writers are just beginning to discover its full potential.

It's a fascinating time, and exciting to be part of it.

How to Use This Book

Are you reading, or listening?

If you're reading, you might prefer to scan-read first, then return to the sections you need. If you're listening, you're possibly doing something else at the same time. So you may want to listen twice.

I've included notes on flow and language strategies. For these, it's probably best to download the PDF from my website, method-writing.com, which has useful words and phrases, as a reference for editing.

Firstly, there's some background on the audio medium, and what's different about it. Then a brief overview of technology, the listening experience, and listeners.

Followed by language techniques that are particularly helpful for audio. This includes words, phrases and structures to use in your writing, whether fiction or non-fiction.

Then, onto narration, and practical ways to help your narrator or voice artist. And finally, some writing and recording tips for if you're narrating your own book.

You can go deep into audio territory, or jump ahead to the section you need most. It's up to you.

INTRODUCTION

A Bit About Me

I'm from Scotland, and I live in a cottage in the Borderlands with my partner. I trained as a journalist with the BBC and Swiss Radio International, and I've done a mix of writing, producing and presenting.

Live radio is pretty hair-raising. Writing to news deadlines certainly sharpens your writing! As does working with tough newsroom editors.

I really enjoyed sound editing, and the ebb and flow of voices – though it was a relief to drop razor blades and move on to digital editing! Much safer for your fingers.

And it was interesting to discover the little tricks that politicians use to grab more air time. They're useful for writers, too!

But my heart was always in storytelling, and now I write fiction as well as plays for stage and radio. And I've learned a fantastic amount from working with directors and actors, about flow, tension, pictures, characters and economy. It's all relevant to audio.

Notes

CHAPTER 1

What's Different About Audio?

Here's a general overview, for orientation. I'll cover each area in detail further on.

New to Audio? Five Key Concepts

Firstly: eyes versus ears
Ears and eyes are very different interfaces with the world. It's useful to know about the physical realities, decoding, focus and other factors that affect how we receive each medium.

Two: listening is linear
Audio moves inexorably forward, like a train on a track. How do you make sure the reader is following the story? Because they can't travel backwards and fill in gaps.

Three: visuals and layout
Non-fiction uses lots of visual elements that help to organise the book or convey complex information. Bullet points, lists. Headers, bold, italics. Images, graphs and tables.
How do you deal with those? You need alternative strategies.

Four: writing flow and structure
How can you use signposts to help orientate your readers?
How do you help readers to get attuned?
How do you create flow to move listeners forward?
How do you make sure they don't get lost when they're hearing something only once?

Finally, the power of performance
How can you help your narrator by writing a performance-friendly script?
If that narrator is you, how can you speed up the recording process?
How can you exploit audio-friendly writing effects such as rhythm?
What techniques can you learn from people who perform for a living?
From this you'll gather that yes, audio writing is different.

Frequently Asked Questions

If you're a writer new to audio-first thinking, and wondering whether to dive in, the next section is for you.

Is audio-first writing complicated?
No. It's just a mindset shift.
Once you've understood the basics, you'll be armed with powerful writing and editing tools for all your books to come.

Can I leave it up to my narrator?
Good narrators will make the best of your book and disguise shortcomings where they can.
But they can't improve the writing and make it audio-friendly.
Get your book audio-ready, make it really fun to perform, and you'll see a big leap in the impact. Your narrators will be able to perform on full power, and your book will be easier to engage with and enjoy.

Do I need this? I'm a literary writer
If your writing is experimental or visual, or reliant on the print medium for its effects, then that's your creative choice.
But if you're interested in the future of books and the potential of multimedia, you may find audio highly inspiring to your creativity.

What's new? I'm a natural born storyteller
Then you're so lucky. Audiobooks have hardly got started, sales are booming, and straight-to-audio fiction is on the rise. If your style is already influenced by oral tradition or you're into spoken word, performance poetry or dialect writing, this is a gamechanger. Get on board!

Is audio-first useful for fiction?
Yes, even if you already write with rhythm and spoken word style foremost. It'll help with clarity, impact and keeping listeners on board. Tactics for flow and order of information will be particularly useful.

Is this useful for non-fiction?
Yes, especially useful. Because print books use visual layout which doesn't easily translate into audio.
Using flow words and phrases and understanding the basic audio concepts will make a big difference.

What do you suggest for writers in a hurry?
Join my mailing list (see p.87) on my website, *method-writing.com* and get the printable tipsheets.
They include a list of transition words, connectives and flow phrases which you can use right away.
Writing an audio-friendly script also cuts costly time in the studio, and will give you a better result.

Will this help with narrating my own book?
Yes. Although the focus here is on audio-first writing, rather than technical stuff such as home studios and recording, I've included tips from my own recording experience, to help you get started and avoid some pitfalls.

Audio-First Writers

Plenty of people in different worlds already write for the ear first and foremost.

After all, it's an old, old skill. You could see audio-first as campfire storytelling by another name.

In a way, we're back full circle to the oral tradition, when people carried and transmitted stories directly from mouth to ear.

Then came along print, which made our stories portable, and allowed us to preserve them externally.

Then came audiobooks on CDs and cassettes – portability and preservation of sound. But still limited distribution.

Now, we have fast digital distribution, tiny portable devices, and people recording studio-quality audio at home.

It's breath-taking. Hours of spoken word can be carried around in your pocket.

So it's worth revisiting those early storytellers, for a sense of how things worked before print came along.

Early Storytelling

Imagine that dusk is falling, and your tribe are gathering round the fire. The storyteller or shaman or bard is waiting patiently. They're an important figure and they're sat prominently, all eyes upon them.

Someone throws more logs on the fire, and sparks fly, illuminating everyone's faces in a red glow. Your family, friends, visitors from a neighbouring tribe – everyone's here for this special night. The storyteller waits till everyone gets settled. A hush descends. And the storyteller begins.

Well, in some key respects, audiobooks are just like that. And in others, clearly not.

Here's what the oral tradition and audiobooks have in common.

Firstly, the experience is linear. It unfolds in time, and is on a track you can't divert. If you miss what was just said, it's too late – it's flown past!

So spoken word needs exceptional clarity. Anything muddy, or in the wrong order, will confuse the audience and have them doing mental backflips.

Oral storytellers use repetition a lot to make things clear. And in oral storytelling cultures, people were often familiar with the stories anyway.

With audiobooks, this is rarely true. So clarity is even more important.

Then, there's the issue of who's in charge.

In the oral tradition, it's the storyteller – the shaman or bard or comedian. It's a skilled performance, carefully planned, and they hold you on track with techniques such as hooks, questions, tension, arcs and rhythms.

Whereas with written books, the reader is in charge. Readers can stop and start, skip around – even right to the end – and wander off at tangents.

And finally, oral storytelling goes directly into your brain. You can drift and dream, but you're still taking it in with your senses.

Whereas with reading, there's a layer of active decoding. It's more active and focused, less direct. The reader is doing far more of the work.

And there's another key area where the oral tradition and audiobooks are very different.

Oral storytelling is usually a group experience, focused on the story and the teller.

Whereas audiobooks are intimate. You usually listen on your own, and do something else at the same time, so focus is split.

Each of these factors has a bearing on writing technique.

Modern Storytellers

Today, there are still modern equivalents to the traditional oral storytellers, and they still use similar techniques:

Performing artists
People who perform in front of live audiences know so much about rhythm, pace and engagement. They include children's and indigenous storytellers, actors, performance poets, spoken word artists and comedians.

Broadcast journalists
They write news stories and features for reading on air, and often present them, too. They learn a lot about transitions, segues, and creating vivid radio pictures.

Scriptwriters for radio, stage or screen
They write for performance by other people, which calls for extraordinary empathy, clarity and economy.

Preachers, orators, politicians
They need to transmit the spoken word clearly at a distance, and harness the power and rhythms of rhetoric.

Audiobook Research

If audiobooks are your target market, you need to research them, just as you'd do with print and ebooks.

On Audible, you can listen to short audiobook samples online – like the Look Inside function in print and ebooks. This will give you a flavour of different voices and styles.

If you aren't already signed up for Audible, do this now, start listening, and take advantage of the free trial.

Listen to books in the genre you write in, to get a flavour of how audiobooks sound in a book style you're familiar with. Fiction and non-fiction use different strategies. Listen out for voices, viewpoint and how sections and transitions are handled.

Take notes on what you discover. If you use Kindle, try out Whispersync and the transition between audio and ebook. Try listening at different speeds, and on different devices, with and without headphones.

Once you've got a good sense of audiobooks in your genre, it's time to move on to the features of the medium itself.

Notes

CHAPTER 2

Audio and Listening

With audiobooks, it's useful to break it down into factors that you, as a writer, can and can't control.

You can't control what your listener is doing, or the technology.

You have some control of things like getting the best from your narrator.

And you can 100% control the writing.

Let's start with the things you can't control.

The Audio Medium

Audio flows forward in a linear way. It's like a train track.

As a listener, if you miss something, you can't easily go back. But you can leave the train. In other words, switch off.

So people in linear platforms such as broadcast have to be particularly skilled at finding good ways to keep the audience involved.

Live broadcast is especially demanding, as your audience can easily switch channels.

The good news with audiobooks is that listeners can at least pause and rewind.

Print and ebooks, meanwhile, are relatively forgiving. If you miss something, you can go back and reread – even years later!

So with books, wandering off is fine. But our eyes even wander during reading itself.

When we read, our eyes make jerky movements called saccades – short stops or fixations, followed by tiny jumps in the text.

Eye trackers have shown that we read in little clusters of words, with an expanded field of vision. So we're often taking in words and impressions round the edges, even if we don't realise it. We're picking up context and genre signals and filling in gaps as we go along.

So if you forget the name of the heroine, or who a pronoun is referring to, you may well scan the page, refresh your memory and return to the sentence without even blinking.

Imagine a terrier on a path, stopping to snuffle, then jumping ahead. There's comparative freedom and choice.

Whereas an audiobook is like that train track.

What are the implications?

Firstly, clarity is paramount. If a listener is confused, they may switch off.

Secondly, forward momentum and drive really help. That's where hooks, arcs, foreshadowing and transition words come in.

Finally, the listening experience needs audio ebb and flow to create interest. The narrator's performance is one factor, but it also needs structuring techniques built into the writing, including an awareness of rhythm, pace, emphasis and intensity.

Technology

Technology is another factor beyond your control.

Audiobooks aren't in high quality audio. They're digital files compressed small enough to be streamed or downloaded. So they don't have the sparkling detail of a live performance, or even a CD.

Further along the chain, you don't have control of your reader's listening device, either.

With voice activation on the rise and new cars being equipped with the internet, audio delivery platforms are still evolving fast.

The good news is that ears are pretty forgiving and can tune in to what's offered. They can focus, a bit like camera lenses.

But they can't improve a poor-quality audio recording. So when you record, it's good to strive for the best possible quality.

How to ensure audio quality?

That's a job for your sound engineer. They should know about editing, compression and processes to record and optimize your sound.

But how can you tell if your great-sounding studio recording will come across well through someone's tinny earbuds?

Here's a tip from radio sound engineers.

When I worked in radio, the sound engineers had amazing state-of-the-art equipment.

But what did they use to really test programme quality? The smallest, cheapest, tinniest speakers you can imagine.

I saw them sitting on a shelf, no bigger than a dictionary, and pretty battered and dusty-looking.

The sound engineer explained: 'If it works for listeners with terrible reception, huddled round a tiny shortwave radio in a remote part of the world, then it really works. That's the acid test.'

So, if you want to know whether your audio is clear enough, listen through cheap speakers or earbuds.

Platform

Again, you have no control here, and need to know what you're dealing with. Currently, by far the biggest audiobook platform is Audible. Google Play and Apple iBooks are next in scale.

For authors, it's important to know that Audible is an Amazon company.

If your audio is on Audible, it's part of the biggest book sales ecosystem on the planet. Amazon ebooks, print books and audio all cross-promote and upsell to each other, and listeners are far more likely to find it. So it makes sense to be part of it.

Authors can choose between going exclusive to Audible, or "wide" – that is, available to other platforms. There are pros and cons either way, and this, too, is evolving fast, so it's best to check the latest state of play online.

But one game-changing feature of the Amazon ecosystem is *Whispersync*.

Whispersync synchronises the audio and ebook versions of the book, to create a seamless "immersive reading" experience.

Say, for example, you're reading the ebook at home, then head out in the car. Using Whispersync, you can continue with the audio version, without losing your place. Then back to the ebook.

What does Whispersync mean for writers?

To qualify for Whispersync, the audiobook needs to be an exact reflection of the e-book. The text needs to be pretty well identical, for the syncing to work.

When I recorded my first audiobook, it felt natural to add in flow words – things like *so* and *next up*. This is standard for smoother transitions in radio.

But it made my audiobook incompatible with Whispersync.

Audible Whispersync

For future, I decided it made more sense to start with the audiobook script, and create the print book from that.

Then I wouldn't need to adapt the book later.

It has meant adopting a slightly different writing style, and you may not want to do this.

But it's worth being aware that audiobooks are influencing how people write.

What are the implications?
You may want to edit your existing books to make them more audio-friendly. Or, you may want to move on and write audio-first for the next book.

It depends on whether you consider Whispersync to be important for your books and market.

Listeners

Listeners, too, are outwith your control, and they're a very varied bunch.

But the listener you know best is *you*.

So have a think about your listening habits. Do you multitask? Do you listen randomly, or choose specific books or programmes? Do you have good focus, or does your attention dip in and out? Do you listen for entertainment, inspiration or information?

You'll probably find your listening habits have changed quite a bit in recent years. Here's a snapshot of mine.

I listen to audio for entertainment mainly when I'm in the kitchen, doing the washing up or ironing. I'm multitasking. I may be clattering dishes around, or switching in and out of the room.

If I'm listening for information or education, I'll probably stay in the room. Sometimes – and you might find this alarming – I speed up information podcasts, to listen faster.

What's changed? These days, I rarely listen to the radio in the car. More usually, when I'm in the car, I listen to chosen music or to podcasts on my smartphone.

How about you?

Human variation

And finally, human individual variation is also out of your control. Our individual ears – big, small, flat, sticky-out, hard of hearing, super-sharp – differ greatly in how they listen.

Ears can focus, just like a camera lens. Your brain tunes into things it finds interesting. Attunement is very important for audio-first writing.

Often, our ears are in soft focus, and drift in and out of attention. Sometimes, they snap into super-alert HD focus.

Remember the cocktail party effect? When you're in a crowded room and suddenly hear your name across the far side?

Your brain has learned to tune into things that may be significant for you, such as your name or town, or meaningful phrases.

It can also tune out insignificant background noise, such as general traffic or the wind.

If we didn't do this, we'd be wrecks from living in a hyper-vigilant state all the time.

So for most people, listening is a mix of casual drifting, and moments of intense concentration when they pull focus.

And this is personal to each listener and the context.

What are the implications?

Listeners often multi-task and have a split focus. They're often listening on their own.

And they have highly personal reasons why certain things chime for them.

So to sum up, while we'd all love to imagine devoted readers in quiet locations, concentrating on our every word, in practice, this isn't likely.

One school of thought is that it's better to imagine your listener as a distracted, slightly deaf reveller in a noisy pub.

Or someone in a distant country, listening to a crackly short-wave radio.

Extreme? Maybe.

But it does bring home the need for clarity.

CHAPTER 3

Visual Book Elements

Visual book elements are tricky for audiobooks. That includes graphs, images and tables, for example. And structuring elements such as bullet points, lists and headers.

The best approach for your book depends on your genre and content.

Fiction is easier than non-fiction here. A few chapter headings won't detract from your listener's immersion in the story world.

Non-fiction often uses graphs, tables, sections and bullet points to structure a hierarchy. This is hard to get across in audio.

So, here are some strategies for some typical visual elements found in books.

Large Graphics

Audiobooks can't include large images, tables and other useful illustrative material from the print version. This may seem a problem, but it can be turned into a plus.

If you have material like this, consider making a PDF and providing it as an online download. This can be posted on the Audible platform along with your book, or on your own site, giving you another way to connect with readers.

This provides extra value, and is useful for any material likely to go out of date, such as a reading list, or a list of technical equipment.

It'll also help to future-proof your audio recording. Instead of having to update both ebook and audio every few months, you can simply update the download.

You can also consider downloads if your book is fiction – say, a map of your story world, or pictures or family trees of your characters.

Again, this adds value to your audiobook, and gives another way to connect to your audience.

Statistics and Graphs

Basic statistics and graphs can be expressed in words, by using comparisons or analogies.

For example, let's say you have a graph showing a sharp rise in the number of tree sparrows in Scotland. Try replacing it with a sentence:

> ***The number of tree sparrows has almost doubled in 20 years.***

Metaphors and analogies can also be used to create vivid pictures:

> ***The plot of land was the size of three football pitches.***
> ***You could fit three London buses into the room.***

Radio stations in the UK are fond of phrases like "the size of Wales", or "the size of four London buses". But sometimes, comparisons can be meaningless to an international audience.

If the comparison is culturally specific, it may need to be adapted, depending on your book's audience.

Numbers

In writing for the ear, the convention is to round figures up or down. Long numbers are hard to take in anyway, as you'll realise if you've ever tried to remember a phone number on the hoof.

So don't say *39*, but round it up to *nearly 40*. Not *105*, but *more than a hundred*.

Note that in radio writing, journalists often avoid *over* as a synonym for *more than*, as over has a spatial meaning, too.

> **MORE THAN 3,000 *people turned up at the demo.***
> ***The writers sold MORE THAN *a million books at the conference.***

Another radio technique is to express numbers by using analogies.

For example, rather than saying the stone was 4 inches across, you might say it was *as big as her hand*. Or, the alien was *four times the size of an average human*.

Analogies have the advantage that they also create images, which help listeners to see the story more clearly.

A third technique is to avoid the number and instead, evoke an impression of what the number means – in other words, its emotional impact. For example, rather than saying *hundreds of bees*, you might say *a great swarm of bees*.

Depending on your genre, the literal meaning may not be important or even that clear to listeners. A word-picture can create a more powerful impact.

Structural Elements

In non-fiction, visual elements such as headers, bullet points and lists are often used to create the hierarchy of the book.

Visual hierarchies are great for print and ebooks. They really help with information clarity, and speed of understanding. But they rarely work in audio.

With audiobooks, it's often better to avoid hierarchical elements where possible, and instead, concentrate on flow.

Here are some ways to approach different structuring elements:

Titles and section headers

Major headers such as chapter titles can be left as they are. They provide a clear signpost, and also refresh the rhythm of reading with a new point of attack.

Section headers are fine, too, as long as there aren't too many.

Too many smaller sub-headings don't work so well. If your narrator is reading out a new section heading every few paragraphs, it can create a stop-and-start effect that compromises flow.

It can also sound a bit formal. Chapter headings simply aren't a natural way of talking to someone.

With headings, it's also hard to get across nested hierarchies or sub-sections. The reader can lose sight of the overarching shape and what's important.

So use headers for large sections such as chapters, but keep an ear out for too many sub-sections.

Bullet points & lists

Lists and bullet points sound indistinguishable in audio, and they can be pretty monotonous. Numbered lists are sometimes used in non-fiction – say:

1. Oranges
2. Apples
3. Pears.

But it's better just to flow a short list together – oranges, apples and pears. If it's a long factual list needed for information, put it in a PDF download.

Numbers are fine, however, when they're used to signpost longer paragraphs, as in "first, second, third". This helps the flow and creates a sense of shape. This is covered later in the section on flow.

Typography

Typography includes elements used for emphasis, such as italics, bold and underlining. These can sometimes be useful in giving a steer to narrators for their performance, and can often be left in.

However, before you go overboard with underlining, bold or italics, check in with your narrator about their preferred approach. Some professionals may be distracted by too many suggestions, and prefer their own reading rhythm.

Note too that underlining is easier to spot in a script than italics and bold.

Quote marks and dialogue

Quotation marks that signal dialogue can be left in, as a steer for your narrator.

But avoid ironic quotations marks – for example, "the expert", implying the person wasn't an expert. Instead, use "the so-called expert" or "the self-styled expert".

In fiction, you may be able to cut a lot of dialogue tags, such as "he said". The narrator will be voicing the different characters in any case, and that may be enough to keep clear distinctions.

Web Elements

Website names are notoriously cumbersome to say on air. The "www" element alone is quite a mouthful.

Keep web addresses tight and snappy by dropping the "www" element – for example, "bbc.co.uk" or "method-writing.com". The hyphen there isn't ideal, but still workable.

Long, complicated URLs are best avoided entirely. Save them for your download, or use the navigation path if it's not too long. For example, "method-writing.com, in the Downloads section".

If you have an ebook with lots of website links, decide whether you want it to be eligible for Whispersync. If you do – and most writers will – it's probably best to cut URLs, and compile them into a PDF download.

Flag this up at the start of your audio recording, with a reminder at the end.

So, that ends the section on visual book elements.

The next chapter is equally important for fiction and non-fiction writers, and will help you to structure your writing for greater audio impact.

CHAPTER 4

Writing for Flow

By now, you've got a picture of an imperfect medium, and an imperfect listener. Don't panic! It's just a wake-up call about clarity.

Did I say that clarity is the main consideration in audio writing?! Other than that, you have two main jobs:

Get the listener's attention, and sustain it.

This brings us onto "flow" – the art of shaping the listening experience as it unfolds.

Some flow techniques will be familiar, such as hooks and questions. Others, such as attunement and foregrounding, may be less familiar. Others are rhythmic and part of the art of rhetoric.

They're all writing patterns that can help to shape storytelling, and pull the reader through.

You're probably familiar with large-scale writing patterns such as story arcs, and rising and falling tension. But there are similar patterns at the smaller scale of paragraph level and sentence level.

Learning to use them will help your audio flow and clarity, and make you a ninja editor in general.

What is Flow?

It's helpful to imagine language as a stream. It moves forward, in a linear way, stopping and starting as it goes.

You can get some sense of language flow by looking at punctuation.

Full stops, for example, create a short pause – a bit like a rock in the stream.

Commas are more like pebbles which create just a slight bump.

Ends of chapters are like an obstacle that halts the storytelling temporarily.

And within sentences, you have word clusters and phrases that are like swirls and eddies.

We experience these unfolding shapes physically and emotionally, as an ever-changing pattern of tension and release, rise and fall.

Flow is a kind of music. But not the musicality of the narrator's voice.

Rather, the musicality of language structure itself. Paragraphs, sentences, words and how they're shaped to pull the reader through.

How do you build sentences and paragraphs for optimum flow?

That's the topic of the next section.

Writing Techniques

Flow words and phrases are a bit like the glue that keeps the sense of writing together. They're formally called *connectives* or *conjunctions*, from the Latin word for *to join*, since they join together the other parts of speech.

As a basic example of flow, think of the phrase "on the one hand".

It's usually followed by "on the other hand".

If it isn't, we feel frustrated, because the first phrase is part of a larger structure. There's a setup – *on the one hand* – and a progression – *on the other hand*. Both parts are needed for a satisfying flow.

It's a similar structure to "question and answer", "call and response", "verse and refrain", or even "plant and payoff", in story structure.

You might think of the structure as a rising shape, followed by a falling shape. The first creates an expectation, and the second satisfies it.

There are lots of structures like this in language.

"Firstly," is usually followed by "secondly". "There are three aspects to this question" is usually followed by – you've guessed it – the three aspects.

"If" is often followed by "then", as in: "if you don't take an umbrella, then you'll get wet".

The effect is similar to a story hook, but it's made of language structures.

Language structuring techniques like this can be used to help create arcs of attention – just like story arcs, except at a smaller scale. And this shapes the listening experience.

This is very similar to patterns in music. The verse of a song creates the expectation of a chorus. And if you've ever played a 12-bar blues, you'll know that it has a particular journey or arc which rises and falls over 12 bars, and then often has a bridge that flows the music forward into the next 12 bars.

So, having established that there are different language shapes for getting and sustaining attention, let's look closer at the first kind.

Getting Attention - Openings

Openings are crucial, as they're the point where readers engage with your writing. It's an emphatic position that commands attention. *Listen up!*

In music, you might refer to the "attack" of a note or phrase, which is how it starts, as opposed to "sustain", which is the durational element.

The grandparent of all opening phrases is "once upon a time". *You're about to hear a story.*

"Hwaet!" or "hark!" said the old Anglo Saxon storyteller, as families settled around the campfire to hear the monster saga of *Beowulf*. "Hwaet! Lend your ears!"

These words are a kind of hook to catch the listener's attention.

And they're both very important, and surprisingly unimportant. Here's why.

Introductory words

With audio, your very first words are for tuning your listener in. They don't need to carry much meaning.

Think of the phrase "once upon a time". It doesn't mean much. It just signals that a story is about to begin.

What counts is what comes next:

> *Once upon a time there was A PRINCESS*
> *Once upon a time there was A DRAGON*
> *Once upon a time there was SMALL GIRL WHO WANTED TO VISIT HER GRANDMOTHER*

Listen! A story! About a small girl and her grandmother.

The first few words are like a musical upbeat – the intro before you land on the main beat.

The important meaning comes in the next few words.

That could be the main character – the princess, the dragon.

But it could equally be the setting.

> *Once upon a time there was once A DARK WOOD where no light got in.*
> *There was once A HOUSE ON A PRAIRIE.*

This kind of intro phrase isn't just used in fiction – it's just as common in non-fiction.

When I worked in a radio newsroom, we used a whole bunch of intro phrases at the start of news stories. And not just at the start of the bulletin – at the start of each story.

For example:

> *Moving on now to domestic issues...*
> *Staying with international trade...*
> *And in other news...*
> *Meanwhile...*

Often, news stories can be as little as 20 seconds long, and each one needs a fresh attack. So these apparently meaningless signposts have an important flag-waving job to do.

And as with fiction, the significant element lands not right at the start, as you might expect, but in the next few words. Like this:

> *And in other news, AN ESCAPED PANDA...*
> *Meanwhile in Birmingham, A COUPLE have been arrested...*
> *And in other science news, A TOTAL ECLIPSE...*

Why is this? Because of a factor very important in audio writing:

Attunement

Attunement or "tuning in" doesn't mean dialling to the right station. It's the time it takes for listeners to engage with a voice. To pull focus. To get their ear in.

If you've done meditation practice, you'll be familiar with attunement. In a room full of people, it takes a little while for everyone's attention to settle where it's meant to. So the group leader allows a little time.

Listening to audio is similar.

Tuning in only takes a few seconds, but those seconds are vitally important.

Firstly, voices are highly varied, and it can take a little while to get used to someone's style of speaking.

The narrator may have a different accent or dialect, a different speed, pitch or delivery than you're used to.

So these phrases act as a kind of voice taster, helping the listener to settle in.

And secondly, listeners drift. Their attention may have wandered to something else. They may need to be pulled into a new zone of focus.

And thirdly, you may want to signal a new opening, a fresh point of attack. Maybe a new chapter, or a change of scene. Or simply a different news story.

Listeners need a moment or two to transition mentally, whether to a new voice, or a new topic. Transitional phrases help to carry them along more gently, tuning their ears in.

If transitions are too quick, they can sound odd, even comedic. Like this:

...THE FUNERAL *takes place on Friday.*
AN ESCAPED PANDA...

If one story is sad and the next quirky, the transition is too abrupt, and doesn't allow any adjustment time – either for the listener, or the speaker.

You'll often hear experienced radio presenters naturally pause to create a space for transition, or use a transitional phrase.

This feels necessary for rhythm and flow, and is one of the main differences between audio and print.

Attunement is one reason why writers need to work particularly hard on openings. And it applies equally to fiction and non-fiction.

So, how might you use this?

Look at the openings of new chapters and sections. Identify the main words that carry the most important meaning.

Try to place them not right at the start of the sentence, but a few words in, to allow room for attunement.

Attunement in fiction

The idea of attunement can also be used to develop your fiction openings further.

The listening human brain can only hold so many ideas at once. Overloading listeners with too much story detail can simply overwhelm them.

So you need to choose what to focus on in those crucial first moments.

I like to think of story openings as like cog wheels. The reader needs to engage properly and securely, to create traction that carries them along.

If not, it can feel like a bicycle with slipped gears. You can slither along, miss bits, and never feel secure in the story.

In the hands of a skilled storyteller, you feel confidently engaged from the start, with just the right balance between clarity and intrigue.

One way to achieve this is to narrow your focus right down in your opening, to very few elements.

You can then develop these elements in more detail. But first, they need to be firmly established in your listener's mind's eye.

Three key elements

When you write a story, you need to paint a picture for the reader. With audio sweeping by so fast, the broad strokes of the picture need to be established even more quickly.

A bit like a rough outline or a silhouette. Something just for orientation. The details can be filled in later.

It can be helpful to shoot for only three elements: say, the character, the location, and how they're connected.

> *A POLICE OFFICER lying down in A STREET.*
> *A WOMEN in A FIELD with A DOG.*
> *A CHILD sitting on A SWING.*

With these simple elements, readers already can already create a strong visual image.

This kind of starting point gives our minds a basic picture to hold onto. We can fill in the rest over time.

We don't need to know right away that the child has short brown hair and a green anorak, or that the policeman has a shotgun wound to his right temple.

That level of detail can come in the second or third sentences, or later in the story.

But for orientation, especially with audio, it's helpful if some clear visual building blocks land right at the start.

It's amazing how whole stories can be evoked with just three elements:

> ***A MAN, A BOAT, A BIRD** – The Old Man and the Sea.*
> ***TWO WOMEN in A CAR** – Thelma and Louise.*
> ***A MAN, A BOY, A ROAD** – The Road.*

This works at scene level, too. Think of the sentence:

> *Josh rode up to the ranch.*
> **JOSH – RANCH – RODE UP.**

There's an image of Josh on a horse, heading for the ranch. He's male, on a horse, in a specific setting. We don't know if he's young or old, but for now, we have a general picture.

> **SUSAN – BUSHES – GUN.**

There's an image of Susan in the bushes with a gun. What she looks like and who she is can be fleshed out bit by bit.

> **WINDOW– CURTAIN – EMILE.**

There's Emile at the window, next to the curtain.

We don't know what he's going to do – swish it aside, or hide behind it? But we at least have a picture of the basic setup, and can start forming a picture in our mind's eye.

So, check your chapter openings and see if the key visual elements land effectively, using simple vocabulary. Don't over-describe with complex vocabulary and variation until the main concept has registered.

Opening edits

The idea of *three key elements* can also help with editing your openings.

Remembering the need for attunement and orientation, check that each element is clear and provides a firm foundation for engaging your listener. Then they won't have to change their emerging mental picture further down the line.

Say, for example, you write a story opening:

> ***Artona is heading home.***

Let's assume Artona is the main character. However, Artona as a name doesn't tell us anything. It doesn't have any clues about gender, age-specific or even species. But readers will start to form an image. Maybe they'll imagine a rugged male character. Or a six-foot blue, willowy female.

> ***Artona is heading...***

Heading, again, isn't specific. Artona could be in a car, a bus, on foot, or in a spaceship. Readers will create wildly different images.

> ***Artona is heading home.***

Home is another non-specific word. Again, it will conjure very different associations for readers.

So you have three elements which are indeterminate and wide open to all sorts of different pictures, from the rugged man shouldering a club, to the six-foot blue tentacled creature in her spaceship, to the small child in a buggy.

What if your sentence goes on:

Artona is heading home to his tipi on a skinny piebald pony?

All the other versions of Artona have immediately imploded. The readers' mental images have burst like bubbles. They quickly need to create new ones in their place. They're essentially overwriting what they've imagined.

With book reading, this kind of unravelling and rebuilding isn't so much of a problem. Your eyes read in saccades, and absorb clues from words round about, on the edge of vision. You'll pick up a sense of that piebald pony, and know the story world isn't a supermarket or a spaceship.

But with audio, the listener is following a track. If a picture is half-formed and new information comes along, it has to be overwritten.

So specificity and the order of unfolding information is much more important.

You can use the idea of three key elements to check in with your opening words. Are they clear and concrete, or generic? What do they evoke, and do they signpost enough for the reader to start forming a picture that won't need to be overwritten?

To recap:

Listeners can't process a lot of new information at one time.

Give them two or three key elements for orientation, and make those really clear in the opening.

Look for a simple configuration of three nouns that capture the essence of a picture.

If it helps, imagine a poster or Lego figures, or seeing the scene with your eyes half shut.

This is important not just for the very start of your novel or story, but also for each chapter opening, and any new scenes and sections within chapters.

Each of these calls for a mental leap by the listener, especially if you're taking them to a new location, time, character or viewpoint.

And remembering the idea of attunement, it's not the very first words – it's the next few that really count.

So, for example:

> *It was a wild, windy night as Josh rode up to the ranch.*

What's important here isn't so much the wild and windy night – you can write more about that in the next sentence. It's the picture of the character, Josh, as he rides up to the ranch.

Opening words - non-fiction

When it comes to opening words for non-fiction, you'll have your own favourites. *So* has become ubiquitous in the last few years, to the point of becoming unpopular, but it's a very old usage – a bit like the Anglo-Saxon *hwaet!*

In linguistics, this type of word or phrase used for managing conversational flow is called a "discourse marker".

Listen out for the words you habitually use, and find some more unusual ones by listening to others in conversation.

Here are a few examples:

> ***Now***
> ***So***
> ***Once, there was***
> ***OK***
> ***Here's the thing***
> ***The thing is***
> ***Right***
> ***Well***
> ***You know***

> *Of course*
> *Anyway*
> *On that note.*

And on that note, let's move on from "getting attention" to the next stage of flow...

Sustaining Attention - Middles

Once you've got your listener's attention, you next need to *sustain* it.

Of course, your book has a compelling story or engaging information as a starting point.

But what about the language? Are you making the best of flow structures to carry your reader along with you?

Opening phrases can help to revive the listener's interest.

But not everything you write is a fresh start, or a new chapter or section.

For middles of sections and sentences, you need other strategies.

Two useful strategies for audio are what I call *spans* and *foregrounding*.

They're both kinds of signposting that help to sustain attention.

Spans

Language spans or arcs are phrases that sustain the flow of attention over time.

It's useful here to think of the phrase "attention span".

"Span" recalls the span of a bridge, perhaps stretched out across a ravine.

Language can create spans of attention.

As already mentioned, if I say "on the one hand", I'm starting a span which reaches out to connect with "on the other hand".

If I say "firstly", I'm starting a span which will link to "secondly", and maybe "thirdly" and "finally", where it will come to rest.

This kind of connective language is a key element in creating flow.

Flow and the Zeigarnik Effect

The Zeigarnik Effect is a term in psychology that describes the human brain's need for closure.

If we start an activity and don't finish it, our subconscious minds feel slight tension. The tension is only released when the activity is finished or closed off.

Language structures such as "on the one hand" can activate the Zeigarnik Effect.

If we don't get "on the other hand", the loop is still open, which just feels wrong and unsatisfying.

So using arc structures is one way to sustain attention, by exploiting human psychology.

Be warned, though, that the Zeigarnik Effect can also be abused.

In my radio days, I often used to interview experienced politicians who had done media training.

Obviously, they were keen to get maximum air time, and had some tricks up their sleeves.

If you asked them a question, they'd often lean forward and say,

> *"Well, there are three aspects to that question. Firstly..."*

It was a powerful trick, because they'd set up a long arc which was hard to interrupt.

I'd have to forcibly jump in and stop them, which felt pretty rude on a local radio station.

An arc like this creates a kind of expandable vessel for an expounding politician to fill with words.

And it's also really hard to chop during the edit, because it comes with a rising inflection which needs to fall at the end, or it doesn't feel complete.

So that caveat aside, use flow phrases to shape words into bigger chunks of meaning that carry forward. But don't overdo it!

Forward flagging

Most flow phrases point forward in time. They're a verbal signpost that says "something is yet to come". As in "on the one hand... on the other hand".

Here are some other examples of "forward flagging".

> *There are three aspects to this.*
> *There are pros and cons here.*
> *Let's look at the facts. Firstly...*
> *There are different viewpoints on this.*
> *Some people think... others think...*
> *As an aside...*

Those phrases suggest a sequence of elements is ahead – possibly even a long sequence.

Other phrases forward flag just a single element

> *Here's the problem.*
> *Let me put it another way.*
> *In other words...*
> *Not to put too fine a point on it...*
> *And now for...*

And some words are small forward flags all on their own. For example, the word "if" is usually paired with "then", or another following phrase. For example:

> *If it rains, we'll get wet.*

> *If you don't do what she tells you, there'll be trouble.*
> *If I hadn't missed the train, I wouldn't have met you.*

As with the politician example, these phrases create a kind of vessel that remains open and expandable until the moment of closure:

> *If I hadn't missed the train, and had to wait three hours at the station with nothing to do except sit in the café, drink coffee and read my book, I wouldn't have met you.*

Other words and phrases like this which can open sentence arcs include:

> *As long as...*
> *If only...*
> *While...*
> *Whereas...*
> *Although...*
> *Unless...*
> *Now that...*

In language studies, these phrases are called "subordinating conjunctions", and they're powerful for forward flagging if used at the start of a sentence.

Backward flagging

As well as flagging forward, it's also possible to flag backwards. Here's an example:

> *So, that was a look at flow techniques.*

See how that helps to round things up? Essentially, it's like a mini summary to close off the section – the Zeigarnik Effect in action.

Then you can move on with a pickup that flags forwards. For example:

> *Now for a list of useful phrases.*
> *Here are some more phrases for flagging backwards:*
> *As we've discussed...*
> *As you've seen...*
> *As already mentioned...*
> *That's that.*
> *That's all.*

Some phrases flag both backwards and forwards, both referring to what's just been, and signalling something about to come. For example:

> *To sum up...*
> *In a nutshell...*
> *To put it another way...*
> *To paraphrase...*

These kinds of phrase are meta-language – about language itself.

Repetition and touches

Once you've planted an element in a reader's mind, it needs to be kept alive. You need to touch base with it from time to time, or it'll fade from the reader's memory.

This is particularly important for visuals, as part of your job as a writer is to help readers to create pictures in their minds.

Say, for example, you've set up three key elements – *Emile, curtain, dog*. Then you go on to describe Emile's kitchen knife and the scar on his left cheek, at some length.

By this point, the dog will have faded from view. The picture in the reader's mind has evaporated.

So Emile's dog suddenly leaping from behind the curtain comes as a surprise. It's a fresh image, because we've forgotten the dog exists.

An element that's important to the story needs to be kept alive with what I call "touches".

This is simple – it's just a case of checking in at intervals. Mentioning the dog, so we know it's still there.

Imagine beads or gems threaded along in a necklace. Or a spark that flares up briefly, then fades. Each gem or spark is a small "touch" reigniting that mental image of the dog, or any element you want to reinforce.

This will help to keep the element salient in the reader's mind. Touches like this can be simple repetition, as in:

> ***The dog growled, her hackles on end.***
> ***The dog licked Emile's hand.***

They can also be more indirect, less obvious.

> ***A low growl came from near his feet. The scent of wet pelt and mud hit his nostrils.***

Indirect touches help to create atmosphere and reinforce spatial relationships as well as the elements themselves. They also reinforce description and emotion.

This is a powerful editing technique. Check in with your three key elements for a scene, and establish that you've kept each one alive.

Visuals are one way to do this, but don't forget the other senses, as they add great richness and colour to a scene, and help to immerse the reader more effectively in your world.

Repetition and touches are particularly important in non-fiction, when you might want to set out a viewpoint, or make an argument for or against something.

They're a useful substitute for visual signals, such as section heads. They help to consolidate the ground just covered, before you move on to the next section.

By the way, note that when it comes to forward and backward flagging, visual and audio vocabulary are different.

In visual print and ebooks, you can use visual and spatial flagging:

> *See the next page.*
> *See below for details.*
> *See above.*
> *Look out for this in the next chapter.*

But in an audiobook, it doesn't make sense to say "see below" or "see Chapter 5". With audio, you're referring to backwards and forwards in time, rather than space.

Here are a couple of alternatives which can be used for both media:

> *Back in Chapter 5...*
> *A while back...*
> *In due course...*
> *Further down the line...*
> *Coming up ahead...*

Which brings us on to a second way to sustain attention:

Foregrounding

Foregrounding is a way to create emphasis, by using contrast to make something stand out. In language studies, it's also called *salience*.

For example, in the middle of an ordinary sentence like this, I might suddenly mention grabbing the kitchen knife.

See what I did there? I created a contrast, partly through the unexpected content, and partly through the *way* it was said.

Putting a significant element at the end of a sentence is also a way to make it stand out more.

Foregrounding is essentially another kind of spotlight or signpost. It helps you to control flow by shaping where attention goes, and its intensity.

Foregrounding is particularly important in audiobooks. As you know, things fly by fast when you're listening. It's vital to make the important elements stand out, because if they're missed, the reader will get confused.

If you make everything equally significant, the effect is flattening and dull. Like a photo where everything is in focus, from the person to the window to the hills beyond.

Your attention doesn't know where to rest, as everything is in the spotlight.

Writing needs an ebb and flow of attention, to keep a reader's interest.

Pattern and disruption

Our brains are geared to notice disruption. Why? Because back in the cave dweller days, disruption could signal a threat. If a sabre-toothed tiger suddenly appeared on the scene, you'd want to be on instant high alert.

At the same time, our brains are soothed by patterns, and make patterns all the time. If we didn't make patterns of the world around us, we'd have sensory overwhelm and be unable to function.

So, to save on brain processing power, we're very good at grouping things. For example, when we see a big group of trees, we learn to give it the label "forest". Then our brain doesn't need to tire itself out with individual trees.

Our brains create patterns and groupings like this all the time, and surprisingly quickly. Here's an example.

> *A woman walked into the room.*
> *A man walked into the room.*

What do you expect to come next? Do you have a sense of logic, that maybe a child, or a dog, or someone else will walk into the room?

Or do you have a sense that something completely different will happen?

It doesn't matter which. What matters is that only two instances already start to feel like a pattern.

So what happens next will either continue or disrupt the pattern:

> *A woman walked into the room.*
> *A man walked into the room.*
> *A ten-foot elephant thundered into the room.*

When writers and especially comedians talk about the "rule of threes", they're talking about this simple pattern – something the brain is innately drawn to.

Pattern and its disruption are another way to create salience – to foreground something. It's all about contrast.

And note that anything can become a pattern and then stop being novel and fresh. Even thrills and excitement. As a writer, you need to be on constant alert for opportunities to create contrast and interest, interspersed with the relative rest of pattern. This creates a lively sense of ebb and flow.

Intensity and power words

Another way to create emphasis is to use intensity. Some words are simply more powerful for attracting a reader's attention than others.

That might be because of their innate meaning – because they express intense force. For example: to *stride* is more forceful in its intention than to *walk*, which is more generic. It also implies an emotional charge.

Or a word might have more power because it's more unusual and stands out. For example, Alissa's *boudoir* will draw more attention to itself than Alissa's *room*.

Intensity can also come from simple repetition, as in the famous example of "fog" in the opening to *Bleak House* by Charles Dickens:

> **Fog everywhere. Fog up the river... fog on the Essex marshes, fog on the Kentish heights, fog creeping into the cabooses of collier-brigs...**

The vowel sound used so often echoes a foghorn.

Or you could use intensifiers such as adverbs: *very, extremely, unusually*, or *bright red*, for example.

Different kinds of words can be used in different ways to create impact and intensity. Here are some strategies:

Nouns

Nouns are incredibly important. The three key element technique mentioned earlier uses nouns. With nouns alone, you can set up a clear picture and a sense of spatial relationships.

I once asked a theatre director for performance tips. He said: "focus on the nouns". In his view, nouns are the most important words in any text.

If the actor lands clearly on the nouns, the general meaning will come across to the audience. They'll get the gist of what's going on, even if they don't get the detail.

This director did a lot of Shakespeare, which takes a while to tune into, as the language is often unfamiliar. Emphasising the nouns helps with attunement.

When you're editing, it can be a useful exercise to take a highlighter pen and highlight the nouns. Do they add up to a clear picture? Do they evoke a single meaning, or several at once? For example:

She saw the bar.

Bar has different meanings. Did she go inside it? Did she lift it and clobber someone? Did she jump over it?

If the prior context doesn't make it clear you mean "bar" as in "a hostelry selling beer", the listeners will have to overwrite their mental picture. Avoid mental backflips, as listeners can't go backwards.

Verbs

As already mentioned, an expressive verb can be more powerful than a bland verb. So, for example,

> **She strode into the room.**

is more economical and emphatic than

> **She walked into the room.**

"Strode" conjures a clearer picture because it includes a strong sense of intention. The sound of the "d" makes a thud on the ear, which reinforces the idea of footsteps. So unlike the general verb "walk", it's doing several jobs at once.

In a similar way, *thud to the ground* is more powerful than *fall to the ground*. *Heave* has more force than *lift*.

And crucially, powerful words are more compelling to say. A performer can give more emphasis to a clear, powerful verb than to a bland one with no emotional intensity behind it. Characters with clear, intense actions can feel more alive, and the narrator can convey this more easily with the right verbs.

Sometimes, writers beef up ordinary verbs such as "walk" or "fall" with adverbs or other qualifiers.

> **She walked purposefully into the room.**
> **He lifted the stone with a grunt.**

But there are two reasons why this has less impact than using a single powerful verb.

Firstly, "strode" is clearer to say than "walked purposefully", which is muddy and cluttered.

Secondly, the qualifier comes after the verb in the sentence, creating a mental backflip. It's more effective to say:

> *With a mighty grunt, he lifted the stone.*

because the emotional impact important for performance comes first.

When you're editing, check verbs and qualifiers, and see if they can be strengthened, or the order of information changed to foreground intensity.

Be careful, though. If you edit every verb so that it's packed with intensity, the writing can feel too rich – like wading through treacle.

Over-dense writing can feel more like a heightened form such as poetry. The flow can become too compressed, and hard to follow.

Choose verbs carefully. Make sure they earn their keep and place them so that the narrator can deliver a high-impact performance.

Signposts and Order of Information

I've already mentioned signposts as important for audio flow.

As you know, connective words and phrases can help to orientate the listener and create spans of attention which pull the audience through.

Another important factor is order of information. How you unfold information in audio has a big impact on comprehension.

To avoid mental backflips, set the larger context first, and then give the details:

> *Deep in the woods, the owl flitted across to the oak tree, a mousetail dangling from its beak.*

Rather than:

> *A mousetail dangled from the owl's beak as it flitted across to the oak tree deep in the woods.*

By the time we've got to the end of that sentence, we've forgotten how the parts connect, as we're not given the context first, to slot things into. Context then detail is easier for the brain to work with than the other way round.

Similarly, in radio writing, the convention is to say:

> *The UK Foreign Minister, Susie Shepherd...*

rather than:

> *Susie Shepherd, the UK Foreign Minister...*

because the political role and context are more important than the individual's name. Imagine the phrase with a name you've never heard of, and you'll see the point.

> *The child actor, Tina Small...*

rather than:

> *Tina Small, the child actor.*

and

> *The shipping magnate Buster Walker...*

rather than

> *Buster Walker, the shipping magnate.*

If you're writing fiction, try setting the scene first, and then drawing the listener's viewpoint closer into the story:

> *The sun was setting over Istanbul as the muezzin began his mournful singing.*

Sentence length

As you've gathered, sentence length in audio needs to be relatively short. That's so that sentences can be performed clearly, and with effective flow.

Sentences which are so very long and convoluted and without any spaces in between them that they can't be read out successfully without an extra breath are a bad idea.

Seriously, any sentence that is more than three lines long and has you collapsing red-faced in a corner at the end needs to be cut in two, or severely pruned. Your narrator will thank you.

"Which", brackets, dashes

A particular culprit in overlong sentences is the word "which". Long phrases with *which*, brackets or dashes are often used to qualify or explain something else. For example:

> *The DOG – which she'd rescued from the cat and dog home and installed in her flat – HAD a rough, tangled coat.*

Whether you punctuate this with brackets, dashes, or commas, the effect is the same:

The qualifier phrase separates the *noun* and its related *verb*.

With the verb and noun so far apart, it's true you're creating an arc of attention. But if you stretch it too far, the connection can break.

For example:

> *The knife, which she stole from the kitchen and which had a worn wooden handle and sharp shiny blade that stuck through the bottom of her soft suede handbag, was heavy.*

Not only do you need very good lungs to read aloud *which* clauses like this, it's also likely the reader will have forgotten what you were talking about by the time you get to the end.

So do your listener a favour and cut *which* clauses right down.

It's often better to rewrite an aside like this, and break it into two or more sentences.

Tenses

The past perfect tense – *she had been down in the basement* – can sometimes cause mental backflips.

For example:

> *He had been down in the kitchen when he heard her rummaging around in the drawer. She had retrieved the knife and put it in her bag before going upstairs.*

Here's another:

> *Although she'd already retrieved the knife before heading up the stairs...*

Woah! What happened when and where? In what order did the events unfold?

Overuse of subordinate clauses can make people's heads go into a mental tailspin.

It's often better to use the simple past, or sometimes the present tense, and unfold events in a linear way:

> *She went to the drawer and retrieved the knife. Then she headed up the stairs.*

Endings

In this overview of writing flow, we've looked at openings – attracting attention – and middles – sustaining attention. Endings are the final piece of the jigsaw, and they have a lot of power.

Along with openings, endings are a key "power position". An ending gives the final impression that resonates with audiences. If they're at a performance such as a stage show, it's the impression they go home with into the night.

So endings have disproportionate impact. They need to be strong, clear and resonant.

Of course, this is true for books and stories, too. You'll want to complete a satisfying arc for your readers, with rising tension, a climax and a falling, resonant moment at the end.

But flow operates at different scales. So endings are powerful not just in complete works, but also in paragraphs and sentences.

This short section is about ways to maximise the power position of endings.

Landing

The end of a sentence or paragraph is a breathing space. There's a moment of silence, which creates contrast with the flow of words. Intonation falls to a point of rest.

In other words, the sentence *lands*.

"Landing" is a really useful concept for writers. I've often heard it used by directors in rehearsal. They might, for example, tell an actor, "that line isn't landing".

In other words, it isn't hitting home clearly, so that it's properly heard, and has full impact.

We've already heard that nouns are important in performance, and need to land properly.

Well, endings are a powerful position for words that need to stand out – for example, the three key elements discussed earlier. Some words are more important than others for the meaning of your story.

But often, I see writing where key elements are buried in a chunk of prose, and almost invisible. For example:

> **She walked up the stairs carrying a knife in her left-hand pocket, clinging tight to the banister as she reached the third floor and saw the lamplight shining under the crack in the door.**

It's possible you didn't even notice the knife in that paragraph. Or that you'd forgotten it by the time I reached the end. And yet it's the murder weapon.

To make the word "knife" *land* effectively, and have full impact on listeners, it needs to stand out. It can't compete for attention with everything else in the paragraph.

Skilled writers shape their writing around key elements which they want to be salient.

They make sure they aren't buried by a clutter of words, and use emphatic positioning to create a powerful sense of music.

So, for example, you might revise that sentence to say:

> **She climbed the stairs slowly, clinging tight to the banister, her hand deep in her pocket, clutching the rusty carving knife.**

In this example, the knife *lands* at the end of the sentence – a prominent position that gets more attention than the middle.

Some of the adjectives have also been cut so that they don't distract – like cutting away weeds.

You could also put the knife in the first sentence, at the end to allow for attunement.

> *Her small suede shoulder bag wasn't made to carry knives.*

And then, you could use "touches" to develop each key element, and create a more vivid picture. In this instance, there's a knife, a bag and some stairs.

> *Her small suede shoulder bag wasn't made to carry knives. Certainly not long steel Japanese fish knives.*
>
> *The wooden handle stuck out three inches, and the sharp point pierced through the soft leather.*
>
> *It would have to do. She clutched the bag and its awkward cargo to her side, and began to climb the stairs.*

Recalling the stairs at the end reinforces the picture effectively, because it shows the character in her context.

Note that poets also use the power of line endings. They can choose to land with the line ending – a so-called "end-stopped line".

Or disrupt the line ending – also called a "run-on" line – which helps to sustain flow.

Poets go further and distinguish between masculine and feminine line endings.

With masculine endings, the line ends in a stressed syllable – for example, the word "knives" or "de-SPAIR".

With feminine endings, the line ends in an unstressed syllable – for example, the word "LET-ter" or "LAND-ing".

Masculine endings sound more abrupt, while feminine endings sound softer and reverberant. Use this to vary the rhythmic effect at the ends of sentences.

Note that although emphatic *landing* is a useful technique, anything that's overused can become repetitive. It's best to use different techniques and vary your rhythms – disrupt the pattern, in other words.

Ever-changing ebb and flow keeps things interesting.

Summary words

And finally, for endings, don't forget those backward flagging phrases which help to round off a paragraph or section:

>*All in all…*
>*In short…*
>*Basically…*
>*Essentially…*
>*In a nutshell.*

CHAPTER 5

Writing for Audience Impact

Most professional writers write for an audience and a specific market, rather than themselves.

You've probably thought about your readers, their interests, and ways of engaging them. And you've probably thought about genre, and read other books similar to yours.

If that's you, you're already thinking in a good direction. Audio is a performance to someone, so audience needs to be high in your priorities as a matter of course.

But attention, flow and foregrounding are only part of the picture.

You also need to think about the nature of your relationship with the audience. Whether close and intimate, or more factual and detached. Authoritative, or friendly, and whether it's about you or them?

This will depend on genre and content, and you'll already have decided these things to a degree when writing. They're part of your voice.

But with audio, extra factors come into play.

Firstly, audio is an intimate medium. You're physically present in people's heads, sending sound waves directly into their brains.

Audio also tends towards the spoken word, rather than the written word. So it's typically a more informal register.

And audio can more directly exploit the sound qualities of words, including poetic and rhythmic effects.

These factors might have a bearing on your writing choices, style and audience connection.

So this section is about writing style, voice and viewpoint, specific to the audio medium.

Narrative Viewpoint

Are you writing in the first person "I" viewpoint? Or 3rd person omniscient? Free indirect style?

These are familiar viewpoint options you have as a writer. Each one has a profoundly different effect.

Some viewpoints draw the reader in close and create an immersive experience, evoking lots of closeup and sensory detail. Others hold the reader at a relative distance by presenting facts or detached description.

Some narrators convey a lot of authority, others prefer to project as a peer or friend, while others are unreliable or playful with the reader.

There's a vast spectrum of different viewpoint options. Tiny changes can make a huge psychological difference.

This will be familiar to you if you've trained in fiction writing, where concepts like "free indirect style" and "psychic distance" are widely taught. It's typically less discussed for non-fiction, but just as important.

Here are some considerations to pull into the mix for audio.

Direct address "you"

The spoken word uses "you" – the second person viewpoint – far more than the written word.

"You" is a very powerful word. It's direct, open, and draws the listener's attention. It creates a sense of direct two-way communication between you and your audience.

It's almost as if you're in dialogue. You have each other's ear.

In many languages, there's a distinction between "you" singular and "you" plural. For example, *tu* and *vous* in French, or *du* and *Sie* or *ihr* in German. This also indicates different levels of formality and status.

In English, there's no such distinction. "You" is the same, whether you're standing on a podium in front of a huge audience, or talking in someone's ear. It doesn't give clues about formality and status.

So "you" can be extraordinarily intimate and emphatic.

It's quite rare to use the second person "you" viewpoint in fiction – maybe because it's so full-on.

Imagine a TV screen where the presenter speaks straight out to you, looking you directly in the eye, never looking away. That's the effect of *you*. If it's overused, it can feel a bit invasive and challenging.

But in audio spoken word forms such as radio, it's very common, because of that strong sense of connection.

It's something to consider, especially if you're writing non-fiction.

How do you see your relationship with the audience? Are you a lecturer, a colleague or peer, a friend?

There may be situations when you want a degree of detachment, authority or formality, in which case "you" might be inappropriate or over-insistent. Maybe you're writing about a personal experience, or a serious topic such as money or health.

There might others when "you" creates a friendlier tone that feels more interactive.

Either way, it's worth knowing that the second person is far more common in the spoken word, and creates a different kind of audience connection. So whether to use "you" is an important parameter to decide when writing for the ear.

Contractions

Another style element typical of the spoken word is the use of contractions – *isn't, won't, can't,* and so on.

Many people have been trained at school to write these out in full – *it is not, will not, cannot*. This is a more formal, literary register, and can sound stiff, if it's not how you normally speak.

But the written and spoken language forms are increasingly converging, and there's no longer such a clear distinction.

I prefer contractions in audio, as they reflect my normal speech pattern.

So, I suggest using contractions if that's your usual way of speaking. It'll sound more natural.

Register

Register is the degree of formality or perceived status of someone's language – whether you, or your characters.

Do you use a lot of long, abstract, Latinate words such as *obfuscate*?

Do you prefer simpler words, such as *confuse* or *muddy*?

Do you use a lot of informal or slang words, such as *mess up*, or *cock up*?

And if you write fiction, what about your characters? What sort of register do they use?

Note, there's no right or wrong here. Different registers are right for different situations and characters. It's likely you use different registers yourself, depending on who you're talking to, and whether it's a formal or informal occasion.

"Code-switching" like this is a natural part of language.

So what about audio?

Well, when it comes to fiction and your fictional characters, everything's up for grabs. They'll have their own distinctive ways of talking, and your narrator will have great fun bringing them to life.

Do they use a high status, formal or technical register? Or do they use a lower status register full of imaginative swear words? That's up to you, and is part of the joy of characterisation.

But what about non-fiction? Does register even come into it? Yes.

Formal, high register language can sound more authoritative, and also a bit more detached.

For example, saying *I concur* instead of *I agree* or *that's right*.

Some high registers are more technical, and full of expert vocabulary or jargon.

Say, talking about an *apiarist* or *apiculturist* instead of *beekeeper*.

This can sound fine if you're talking to other experts, but alienating if you're not.

Registers are a social marker, and can make people feel included or excluded – sometimes described as *in-groups* and *out-groups*.

Slang and dialect words are colourful, and often region-specific, or used only by certain groups. If they're not being used for colour or character voices, you might want to check them in an online dictionary.

It's not about right or wrong ways of doing things. It's about understanding your audience and the relationship you want to have with them.

Do you want to convey authority? Warmth? Confidentiality? If it's fiction, playfulness or unreliability?

Do you want to create an immersive experience, or draw more attention to the writing itself?

These are all high-impact writing choices which it's best to make at an early stage, when writing your book.

Once you've prepared your audio-friendly script, you're ready to record.

Notes

CHAPTER 6

Into the Studio

This section is about the narration of your book, whether by a professional narrator, or by yourself.

All the techniques you've learned about writing for flow and viewpoint will help your narrator when it comes to performance.

When they record, they'll add more colour to your text using their own interpretative skills: emphases and inflections, musicality, rhythm, pace and variation. These are also skills of flow and connection.

Voice artists and studio recording time are expensive, so to keep costs down, it's good to give them as clean and audio-ready a script as possible. Here are some tips to help.

Test Your Script

Always read your text aloud. I do this anyway while I'm writing, and pick up most flow issues and tighten the editing that way.

Nonetheless, I still tweak more when it comes to a final read before the studio.

When you read your text out loud, you very quickly get a sense of anything that's unclear or overwritten. It's also a great way to pick up typos that get missed on a quick visual reading.

And by read aloud, I mean *aloud*.

It's tempting to simply read the text to yourself, either in your own head, or by mumbling it under your breath.

It's best, though, to really perform it out loud, as if you were reading it to someone in the room.

Why? Because it calls for very different projection from reading inwardly.

You won't get a true sense of how it performs, unless you perform it.

Over time, you'll get a better sense of this. But words will still jump out and trip you during performance.

Even after years of reading the news live on air, I always read my script out loud, marking up focus words, and adding slashes to indicate a breath.

I also break up unusual words and write them out phonetically, so they don't trip me up during a live read.

Even simple place names can become tongue-twisters when you're under pressure.

An experienced professional narrator will save a lot of time in the studio by doing this kind of preparation.

Working with a Narrator

Hiring a narrator isn't cheap, but most writers prefer to go this route. If you ever try to do it for yourself, you'll discover that it's a long, arduous and highly skilled process. Professional narrators are worth every penny they earn!

Book narrators may call themselves a *narrator* or a *voice artist*.

Some narrators come from a generalist radio or podcasting background and have attractive, resonant voices that are particularly good for non-fiction.

"Voice artist" is more used by the acting profession, and suggests a wider spectrum of skills, including character acting. If your book is fiction and you need strong characterisation skills, this may be a useful distinction.

What you're paying for is their time. So making your script as tight and readable as possible will help you, too.

Finding a Narrator

You can hire narrators through the ACX platform, or Findaway voices, and many other sources online. A search for "audiobook narrators" or "voice artists for audiobooks" will bring up lots of indie voice artists, and there are also regional specialists for accents – so if you need an American or Scottish accent, for example, use that to refine your search.

All narrator sites should have audio samples showcasing the voice artist reading in different genres.

Look out for a track record that suggests reliability, experience and a specialism in audiobooks.

Listen to at least 20-30 samples before making an approach to your shortlisted narrators.

When looking for a narrator, think of your genre and audience, and don't be seduced too early by wonderful resonant voices.

All narrators have different voice personalities and timbres, and even someone absolutely brilliant may be wrong for your book. It's unrealistic to expect even a trained and experienced actor to be right for every book.

It's essentially a casting job – you're a director looking to fill a role.

Some narrators have a beautiful sonorous voice, but are less skilled at interpretation and characterisation. This is particularly important for fiction. A trained actor will have more range and skill in character portrayal. In non-fiction, too, it's important that complex topics are delivered with clarity and understanding.

Always listen and choose based on what you hear: the audio quality, the interpretation, the performance, the timbre and the emotional impact.

It may be that your book needs a warm, encouraging tone, a sense of authority, or a youthful, edgy voice with an urban vibe. Listen for how the voice will make your listeners feel.

Then choose a shortlist of two or three, and contact them for costs and a short sample reading from your book.

Preparation to Help Your Narrator

A narrator will read your book and do some preparation. They'll scan for tricky words, and research those. They'll ask follow-up questions, clarify tone and characterisation, and probably send you a performance sample for sign-off.

They're unlikely to practise reading aloud every word before going into the studio – that would take hours!

When recording a script, there's always a degree of improvisation – the natural, felt flow of live performance.

A narrator is reading, decoding, interpreting and speaking, all at the same time. It's a complex and demanding job, and calls for tremendous concentration.

So, there are a few things you can do to help, and get a better result in the recording.

As a rule of thumb, it's far, far easier to get the recording right from the start. It's all but impossible to sort out mistakes later on.

If a character name is inconsistent, for example, each mistake needs to be painstakingly re-recorded and edited by hand. But it's hard to get a good match, as even tiny changes in microphone distance change the recording quality.

Make sure you're covered with careful preparation of your own script, and preparation to help the narrator. Ask them about their preferences and workflow, or use the tips below.

Layout

Some narrators read from paper, others from a digital device such as an iPad or laptop screen. Touchscreens have the advantage that they're relatively silent, compared to turning over paper pages. They also save on paper. The downside is they're harder to make notes on.

In the broadcast industries, teleprompters are common, and you can also get free teleprompter apps for laptops and tablets.

Teleprompters help to control pacing. Teleprompter layout also means the text is optimally spaced for reading aloud. As well as being in an outsize font, it's typically broken up sentence by sentence, with even bigger gaps for paragraphs. This gives extreme visual clarity, and a better sense of pace, flow and breathing.

I prefer paper, as it allows me to make notes easily for my own sound editing. I use double line spacing and a 12-point serif font. Large spacing makes it easier to find your place if you lose it during reading, and keep going. I'm less likely to drop a paragraph by mistake.

Your narrator will have their own preferences, so check this out before changing your layout.

Pronunciation

Make a list of any words that may be tricky to pronounce, including character names, place names, and anything likely to be unfamiliar. If you're writing fantasy, sci-fi, or anything historical, technical or set in an exotic location, this is particularly important.

Note that exotic is all about context. Some words may be really obvious to you, such as local place names, but unfamiliar to the narrator. When in doubt, provide the pronunciation.

As well as a written list, provide a voice recording. Just use the voice recorder on your phone or computer, create an mp3 file and send it by email.

The narrator can then use this together with your printed document.

And don't assume anything! When a Scottish cast of actors did a BBC play set in my region, they pronounced the word *reiver* as "ryver". That's the word for those Border outlaws of the 1600s, and it's an everyday word for me. I was surprised they didn't know it, and disappointed they hadn't made the effort to check.

Emphases

You may also be able to help the narrator by adding emphases such as bold, italics or underlining. This can help to avoid ambiguity and allow the reader to tune into the focus of the sentence more quickly.

If it's fiction, you could indicate the different characters by highlighting in different colours.

The narrator will have their own preferences and workflow here, so do check first.

I use extra markup when preparing a script for myself. I find underlining easier to read on the hoof than italics or bold.

I also mark up – and often edit – any word clusters that turn out to be hard to read aloud. Over time, this has also helped my editorial eye and ear.

Narrating Your Own Book

If you've got as far as considering an audiobook, you've probably wondered about narrating it yourself. A narrator is expensive, after all, and everyone has basic recording facilities on their laptop, tablet or phone these days.

I thought that too, and dived enthusiastically in, before I really understood what was required.

How hard can it be? I thought. I have a radio background, I'm quite technical and it'll be fun.

Well, it was tough. A massive learning curve. And I came out the other side with huge respect for audiobook narrators.

It's extremely hard work, delivering audio quality, performance quality, and gruelling concentration for hours on end. Audiobook narrators really do earn those apparently high rates.

And if you do it yourself, you'll need to put in the same work, and also spend on kit to get decent audio quality. Even if you're a natural narrator, it's a big decision.

So before deciding whether to DIY, it's a good idea to consider the business case, and whether it's worth the investment of time and money for your book in general.

How does it fit into your overall author business? Are you likely to recoup the investment of recording an audiobook?

If you only have one book, it's been out for a while and has hit the three-month Amazon dip without gaining much traction, it may be better to wait and go audio for the next book, or even wait till you have a series.

Then you can take advantage of the promotion boost Amazon gives to new books. The two formats can cross-promote each other.

If the investment looks likely to pay for itself, you can still weigh up whether to hire a narrator. Some audiobook services offer royalty share contracts where you and the narrator agree to share in profits. This will cut costs on your side, but most narrators aren't keen, because most books aren't profitable enough.

Another option is to hire a studio and engineer to make the raw recording, and narrate and edit your book yourself.

This will appeal to writers who feel confident about reading and sound editing, but don't want to get into the expense and technical side of recording.

However, studio costs alone are high, and you're still paying for many hours. Mistakes are hard to rectify after the event. Typical small recording studios are generalist and often more used to recording music and bands than long spoken word projects. They may not realise the hours involved.

Book narrators typically have home studios geared to voice anyway, and you're hiring both as a package. So it can be pretty cost-effective.

After weighing up these options, you may still have the bug and be interested in DIY recording. Maybe you're like me – someone who enjoys a challenge and the indie author DIY ethos. In which case, go right ahead!

The next few sections will help you to avoid some of the mistakes I made and raise your game.

Editing for Your Own Narration

Use the earlier editing tips to make your script as performance-ready as possible.

While you're writing, read aloud and make "reading for audio flow" part of your everyday process. Over time, your instincts will become more attuned to the audio medium and this will become natural.

Then, with your script proof-read, prepare it for reading.

Work on paper

I suggest you print out your book. I know – that's a lot of paper!

But if you're like me, you'll discover edits and changes that will feed back into your final ebook and make it better, and it's hard to note these on a screen. It's also easier to note down retakes for the audio editing process. And printed paper can't freeze at a crucial point in the recording.

When I worked in a news studio, we always read from printed paper, double line spacing, left-justified, in a serif font such as Courier.

I would skim-read and make notes:

- Underlining the climax of long sentences
- Underlining the most salient point of information
- Adding slashes for unexpected breaths (though if it's well enough written, you shouldn't need to do this!)
- Adding phonetic transcription of less familiar words, such as *KA-zuo Ishi-GU-ro*
- Underlining tricky words as a reminder to read slowly.

Tablets and touchscreens are evolving, and you may find a workflow that lets you make notes easily on screen. Unlike a commissioned narrator, you also know the material inside out.

So a touchscreen may well work for you. Keep me posted on any tips or apps you discover! Meanwhile, I still work on paper.

Tricky expressions

Often, these can't be spotted until you read aloud. Expressions that look simple can turn out to be unexpected tongue-twisters, or muddy in terms of sound:

> ***assess the situation***
> ***innovative development***
> ***in an interesting way***
> ***the writer's decisions***
> ***the necessary level of analysis***
> ***voice artists***
> ***ACX's stringent tests***
> ***This is .. that's***

They're perfectly normal phrases, but for my narration, they'll need special care – just a touch of slowing down and extra enunciation, so they don't sound garbled. Over time, you'll get to know your personal bugbears and be able to work round them.

Resonant sounds

The sonic qualities of some words and letters are more resonant than others, in certain contexts.

For example, you may find that lots of *s's* and *t's* are a mouthful in close proximity.

Some vowels can also be more easily sustained and carry better than others. For example, *o, a* and *oo* can be given a longer duration than *i* and *u*.

Song writers and lyricists exploit this knowledge by using long vowel sounds for key words in songs. Think of the song *Oklahoma* and compare it with *Ipswich*!

The song *Send in the Clowns* by Stephen Sondheim has the famously hard-to-sing line, "isn't it rich?", with the very short vowel of "rich" in an unusually emphatic position. He wrote it for an actress with strengths in character rather than sustained singing.

When you're doing your performance pre-read, look out for fine edits that will help you to land more effectively on resonant words.

Speaking - Voice Energy, Projection, Speed, Accents

Narrating your own text has challenges, but also advantages. Clearly, you know the content better than anyone, and can deliver it authentically and with authority. You know what you're talking about!

And many listeners appreciate being able to hear the author, rather than a trained actor or narrator. You don't need to be highly polished – any rough edges will make your voice more distinctive and authentic.

That said, we don't often hear our everyday voices as others hear them. What sounds loud and expressive to us in our heads may sound flat and dull to an outside ear. You'll probably need to make some adjustments for your voice to come across at its best in a recording.

Voice energy and projection

Your voice has certain acoustic qualities. If it's already resonant and clear, that's fantastic! But most of us have to do a bit of extra work to get the best from our voice on air.

Firstly, your energy level needs to be higher than normal, with more varied intonation. Think of it as "punching up" the energy, as though you're a slightly more excitable and expressive version of yourself.

Don't force it! This isn't about volume, which can quickly become strained. It's about modulating your tone more, with more rise and fall, and greater clarity of key words. Essentially, you're creating greater contrast, so that the meaning projects more clearly.

It can be helpful to limber up your voice and mouth muscles with stretching beforehand.

This slightly punched-up speaking style will feel a bit unnatural at first. Record yourself and listen back, so that you get a feel for the amount of projection you need to come across well. If you're not used to performance or public speaking, it will be slightly more than you think.

Speed perception

Speed is hard to gauge objectively. Our perception of how fast we speak is unreliable, and we can speed up in excitement or under pressure, without realising how fast we really are. I'm really guilty of this, and have to make a conscious effort to slow down beyond what feels natural.

News anchors typically aim for a reading speed of 150-175 words a minute. You can use this as a benchmark for non-fiction.

Fiction varies more according to the genre and what's happening in the story – whether it's a pacy thriller or a languorous, reflective or seductive scene.

The only way to really test whether your speed works for an outside ear is to record yourself and listen back, and to practise.

It's also worth knowing that many people listen to audiobooks at faster than normal speed. The pitch doesn't rise, so they don't get a chipmunk effect – just a quicker listening experience.

As long as you read in a clear, even way, with plenty of modulation and variety, listeners should be able to tune in and understand you.

Accents

Accents are great, because they bring character and distinctiveness to a voice. If everyone had the same standard English accent, life would be dull indeed.

I'm aware that my Scottish accent sometimes takes a while to get used to, but on balance, I'd rather embrace and celebrate it than attempt something unnatural.

So, if you're like me, and have a pronounced regional or national accent that's less familiar internationally, just take a little more care to speak clearly, and factor in some attunement time.

Recording Tips

The technical side of audio recording is a book all to itself, and that's not the main focus here.

However, as I've worked through the process of learning how to record, I've discovered lots of helpful tips that would've saved time and anguish, if I'd known them earlier. So what follows is a collection of advice I've picked up, which may be helpful if you're going the DIY route, too.

Clean capture

Sound recording has got so much easier and quality kit so much cheaper in the last few years.

However, the quality bar for audiobooks is high. You do need to nail some technical basics if you're going to pass ACX's tests first time round. I didn't, and I have a background in radio! So start with the overview on the ACX site first of all.

The key point to remember is that it's nearly impossible to correct or improve an audio recording in post-production. Always listen to your recording through headphones, as that's the only way to hear what's being picked up by the microphone.

A microphone is super-sensitive. It records everything in its focus, and is very unforgiving. A bit like HD video which, as you may know, isn't too popular with actors, as it highlights every blemish.

A microphone will pick up every noise in your environment: the dog barking down the street, the hum of car engines, the ticking clock, and the echo in the room itself. It'll pick up keyboard noise and the rustle of paper, too. It can even pick up the jangle of your earrings or bracelet, and noises from your teeth.

Each of these sounds is an irritant that detracts from pure voice quality. Some can be painstakingly removed, blip for blip. But that's like painting a wall with grit in the paint, then trying to pick it out. Don't put grit in your paint!

Also, if your recording level is too high and the sound gets distorted at the capture stage, this can't be sorted. It's like recording video with an unwanted wobble. It's in the fabric of the material.

So the message is: control as much of the sound at the capture stage as you can, and make it as clear and clean as possible. That means control of the room, the microphone and the performance.

It can take a while to get the right balance of microphone, external and internal noise and your projection and voice, as it's highly personal. I recommend investing in some time with a sound engineer who can talk you through the options, and let you try out different mic and kit combinations.

Your recording space

Your living room and phone voice recorder are unlikely to be up to the job, unfortunately.

You need a space that's small, and where you can control the sound environment. That's both the sound coming from outside, and the sound inside.

Think of your recording space as like a fish tank. Any leaks to the outside world are problematic.

I have a solo office in a quiet space – at least, I thought so.

But I couldn't control people using the swing fire doors and clattering through. Or the delivery vehicles outside. Or the Crossfit gym people throwing tyres around in the far distance. It shook the floor and sounded like the rumble of thunder.

Back home, I was better able to control the outside noise. I tried the living room, shut off the heating and removed the ticking wall clock. The room isn't that big, but the walls are minimalist bare, so there was lots of echo. The microphone picked up the whole room, which created the wrong ratio between my voice and the surroundings.

About echo

Many people love echo. It can be really flattering for voices.

If you've ever sung in a hall or in a shower with hard, bare walls, you'll know this. You can instantly make your thin voice sound like an angel's, with no effort. If you play the cello badly, like I do, a big echoey hall is magnificent.

But with an audiobook, you don't want to sound like an angel. An angel is a grand, intimidating semi-deity intoning from on high. Not a friend, a peer, an equal.

And as an indie author, you probably don't want a sense of grandeur. You want a sense of conversation, of relatability.

An echoey, resonant space creates a feeling of distance. A small, acoustically dead space helps connection and intimacy.

Echo is present in even small rooms, especially if the walls are bare and there's little to absorb the sound. We're often unaware of this until we hear a comparison.

So do a test. Stick your head inside a wardrobe, snap your fingers, speak and clap, and hear the difference. That's the acoustically dead sort of quality you're looking for. It will give your voice more intimacy and connection.

If you have a decent-size cupboard or wardrobe and can make it comfortable, there's your recording space. If you have the luxury of a walk-in wardrobe full of clothes – bingo!

When I did radio interviews at the local council, we recorded in a cluttered broom cupboard off the main conference room. It was the only way to get decent sound with minimum echo. Don't be tempted to use bathrooms, however small – they're very echoey.

Acoustic treatment

With your small space identified – in my case, a tiny box room – you'll probably need to give it some acoustic treatment to deaden the sound.

Firstly, block off an area if you can – anything that shrinks the size of the space. I use a clothes dryer behind my chair.

Then, deaden any echo by using squidgy materials to absorb echo.

In pro studios, people use wall panels of acoustic foam. Egg packing-type foam does pretty well. But you can also improvise using quilts, towels and cushions.

Use the finger-snap test and move things around till you get the best result. The only way to see what works is to try it out.

Just bear in mind that it takes several days to record an audiobook, so your setup needs to be in place for a good while. You may not want loads of towels and duvets lying around the place.

If you need to shift things around and dismantle during the recording period, take a photo of your setup so that you can recreate it.

Otherwise, the acoustic difference might be audible, and it may be hard to match the recording quality during edits.

Microphone placement

The closer you are to the microphone, the more intimate your voice sounds. Too close, and you start picking up unwanted intimacy such as mouth clicks and saliva sound.

With microphones, the distance effect is highly exaggerated. A tiny change in position can massively change the sound.

So you need to experiment, decide on the sound you want, and stay consistent, or it'll be noticeable during later editing.

For an extreme example of close-miking, listen to one of those YouTube videos of people lip-smacking – it's called ASMR and it's apparently good for destressing.

In between this extreme, and the far-away sound of a narrator way off mic, there's a sweet spot. It'll depend on the type of microphone and your voice and projection, too, so the only way to find this is to experiment.

I have a quiet voice and struggled to find a good combination. The answer in the end was a ribbon microphone, which is rather unusual, but works for me.

Another issue to look out for is the sound of your recording device. Laptops have an underlying hum, and a microphone on a table top can pick up keyboard and clothing noise. As before, listen with headphones on, so that you notice and eliminate these sounds at the start.

Take a note of all your settings and a picture of your studio setup, so that you can easily recreate it next time.

And Finally

It's a fantastic time for audio!

The rollout of superfast broadband and high-speed mobile internet has made audiobooks quick to download.

Radio, podcasts, audiobooks and plays are portable and accessible, and the platforms are increasingly converging.

The BBC has even rebranded its audio strands as *BBC Sounds*, reflecting this change in listening habits.

So it's a very exciting time for authors with an audio interest.

It's especially interesting for writers who enjoy working with dialogue, or oral storytelling, or who come from regional, dialect or storytelling cultures – such as the Scots language – who may not be as well represented as literary English in traditional publishing.

And it's great for writers who enjoy experimenting with musical and rhythmic effects in their writing style.

In short, it's all out there to play with, and it's only just started.

Happy writing, listening and recording!

What's Next?

I hope you've enjoyed this whistle-stop tour of audio-first techniques, and found some useful nuggets to use in your own writing.

If so, here's what to do next.

1. **Leave a review comment** on the platform where you bought the book.

It only takes a minute, but it's a huge help - as you'll know if you're an author or publisher yourself!

2. **Download the free cheat sheet** of flow and connector words and phrases from Method Writing - that's

www.method-writing.com/downloads

And 3...

Join Method Writing!

Join my Method Writing mailing list at **www.method-writing.com** for more tips and resources for writers.

In particular...

Get Your Free Tipsheets

Keep my **Writing for the Ear** tipsheets by your desk for editing. They include connector and flow words, along with genre-specific tips:

- Tipsheet 1 - General Advice
- Tipsheet 2 - Non-fiction
- Tipsheet 3 - Fiction

To get your copies, and a free email mini-course on audio-first writing, join my mailing list at **www.method-writing.com/writing-for-audiobooks-jules-horne/**.

About Jules Horne

I come from the Borderlands of Scotland, home of the Border ballads, so unsurprisingly I've grown up with a Gothic imagination and a gene for storytelling. I write fiction and plays for stage and BBC radio, and perform spoken word as Rebel Cello. I taught on the MA in Creative Writing with the Open University, and helped to write the Script strand.

Join my mailing list (see p.87) to get tips and advice on voice-first writing. I'm an independent author so I'd really appreciate your book review online – it really helps! You can email me directly at **info@method-writing.com**.

www.method-writing.com

Other Books by Jules Horne

HOW TO LAUNCH A FREELANCE COPYWRITING BUSINESS

"Digs deep into the nitty-gritty of the copywriting profession".

Want to get started as a freelance writer for hire? This practical guide gives you the business skills you need to put your words to work.

ISBN: 978-0-9934354-5-4

DRAMATIC TECHNIQUES FOR CREATIVE WRITERS

"A must for any creative writer."

Does your fiction or poetry need more oomph? Give it a boost with dramatic techniques! Discover tips from stage and screen to bring your writing fully to life.

ISBN: 978-0-9934354-9-2

Available from Amazon, Kobo, Barnes & Noble
www.method-writing.com/books

www.ingramcontent.com/pod-product-compliance
Lightning Source LLC
Chambersburg PA
CBHW071019080526
44587CB00015B/2426